Leisure Arts 23

Landscape in Pastel

Aubrey Phillips

SEARCH PRESS

Wellwood North Farm Road Tunbridge Wells

Introduction

I am often asked why I find pastel such an attractive medium for painting landscapes. Its appeal to me lies primarily in its immediacy: after observing my subject and the particular colour I want to put down, I can select the appropriate pastel stick and apply it to the paper without thought of mixing or diluting a pigment. I also like the feel of the pastel stick between my fingers and the direct contact with the paper – there is no brush or palette knife between me and the mark I make. The mark itself is also far more directly transmitted by my hand and fingers – I can press the stick firmly to the paper to make a strong, expressive mark, or skim it lightly across to suggest a wisp of cloud. Another advantage which pastel possesses is that it is a dry medium – I can work freely and fast with it without having to wait for any drying process.

Disadvantages? A few, perhaps, for the novice. Pastels are very superior chalks (in this book I refer to artists' soft pastels *not* to oil pastels or crayons which are greasy) which are a mixture of pure pigment and chalky fillers bound together by gum tragacanth. The paper surface holds with its 'tooth' or grain the pigment mark made. This can easily be smudged. Likewise some people find difficulty in the initial stages in choosing the exact colour from a range of pastels. In both cases, practice overcomes these minor technical difficulties – one keeps sleeves rolled up so that cuffs do not brush across the picture, and one soon learns to lay pastel sticks out in an orderly fashion and choose the appropriate stick instinctively.

Above all, however, I find pastels an unrivalled medium for colour sketching – not only do they produce a vivid spontaneity but I find a benign exhilaration in painting with them. I cannot think of anything more immediately exciting than to complete a landscape sketch to my own satisfaction, having made, perhaps, less than thirty marks on the paper with little more than a dozen different tints and colours. In this book you will see, stage by stage, how I produce sketches and more finished studio work. What both have in common is my delight in using the pastel medium.

Using pastels

When you decide to equip yourself for painting with pastel your first visit to the art suppliers may be a bit daunting. No two manufacturers use a standard by which to designate the colours and hues in their ranges of pastel – what might be 'Yellow Ochre Tint 2' from one maker will probably be quite different both in colour and hue from another. Most manufacturers offer a range of upwards of 200 different tints and colours. Do not be put off. If you are uncertain, buy your sticks individually. You will also find there is a general tendency for darker pastels to be harder than those in the light tints, and each varies from maker to maker. I know what individual sticks to buy through experience.

Some artists keep their pastels in colour range and tint in sectioned boxes: I prefer to strip off the outer wrapping paper (first making a note of the colour and tint on a colour chart) and then break the stick into pieces about one inch long. I keep all my broken pieces in a flour-filled box which keeps the pieces separate and clean enough for me to see the colours clearly. When the flour gets dirty I just tip the box contents into a sieve, get rid of the flour, add fresh to the box and put my pastels back in it.

By breaking up the stick I can make with it both lines and broad blocks of colour by holding the stick sideways. As it wears down it becomes faceted, which provides a further range of marks.

To obtain different effects, you not only use the stick to make the appropriate shape of mark, but by exerting different pressures onto the supporting paper you will see how the paper 'bites' most of the pigment, giving a deeper (or lighter, according to the colour of the paper you use) and more intense mark. Practise making marks on different coloured papers.

Papers

Pastels are used most satisfactorily on tinted papers. The majority of art suppliers will carry a wide range – sugar paper, flock, Canson, Ingres, cartridge. These are soft (flock) through to varying degrees of hardness and texture to cartridge. The colour range is usually quite enticing and offers endless possibilities; but try, when you are painting landscapes, to use a few neutrally toned papers. I use muted greens, greys and buff browns for most of my work.

You can, however, prepare your own by applying your chosen colour in watercolour or thin acrylic to water-colour papers.

When I am working in the studio I stretch my Canson or Ingres papers onto a drawing board with a thin wad of newspaper between them. I soak my paper in water, dry it off with towels until damp, then lay it over the newspaper-padded board and tape it to the edges with gummed strip paper. When dry, the paper will be taut over a cushion of the newspaper, which now has a pleasant 'give' when I apply the pastels to it.

Scottish glen: demonstration

I made a study just as the clouds were lifting from the mountains in north-west Scotland one April morning and when the sun was shining after a period of rain. It was a joyous and uplifting experience to see the blue sky and the sun shining through light clouds.

Stage 1 (page 4)

I select a sheet of light-grey Canson paper, Moonstone tint, and set to work with light tones of burnt sienna, cerulean blue and red-grey pastels, blocking in the basic tints for the sky, with pieces about one inch long, sweeping them across the paper. I indicate the tones of some of the mountains with a stroke of cool grey.

Stage 1

Stage 2

Stage 3

Stage 4

Stage 2

With the cool grey I indicate the basic shape of the glen, and the position of the burn flowing through it, sweeping boldly across the foreground, with a mid-toned burnt umber. I then strengthen the shapes of the near slopes and roughly indicate the buildings, using a dark autumn brown shade.

Stage 3

I shape up the distant and mid-distant mountains with light and mid-tones of cool grey, then with a dark autumn brown and a mid-toned brown, I draw in more strongly the near slopes and add more mid-toned burnt umber to the foreground.

4

Stage 5 – the finished painting

Stage 4

I indicate reflections in the burn from the light sky with pale ultramarine, and with pale brown suggest the light in the middle distance to the left of the buildings. The rocks in the burn are also strengthened.

Stage 5 – the finished painting

I now go over the whole of the picture, emphasising shapes, and with a black conté crayon firm up the drawing of the buildings and the rocks in the foreground. I also add a little mid-toned olive green in this area. I further develop the distant and middle distant mountains, shape up the clouds, and the effect of the light from them on the slopes in the left middle distance.

I prefer to leave this picture as a finished sketch, having achieved the quality that I particularly wanted from the subject – spontaneity.

5

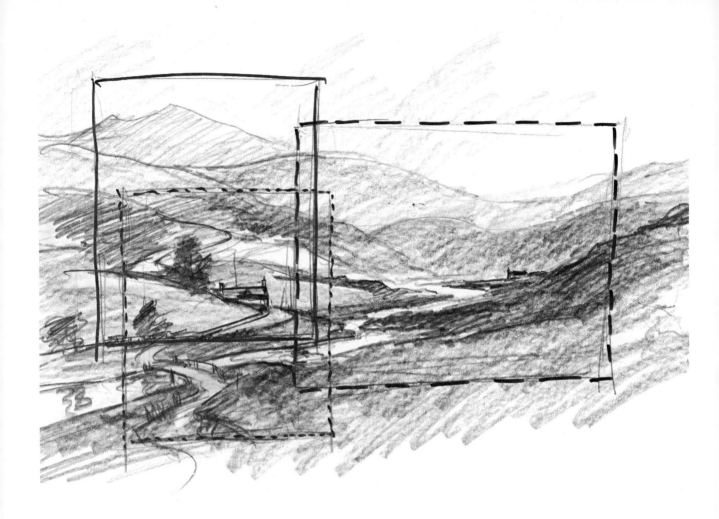

Composition

Always one of the most important considerations in any painting, composition is vital to most landscape studies. Too often I see my students sit down in front of a landscape subject and start to draw and paint straightaway. When they see me making several compositional sketches before I start, they take the point! Above is a panoramic sketch I made beforehand for the demonstration on pages 3–5; as you see, I could choose three separate studies from it, the one finally selected is enclosed by the heavy dotted line. Balance your shapes and masses, both linearly and tonally; and find lines that lead into the centre of interest and not away from it.

When you have flat, relatively uninteresting landscape before you, try to find one strong centre of interest from which the rest of the picture can devolve: a high tree, building or church spire. A brook or river wandering through a subject can provide interest, so long as it does not wind from the centre of your picture to the

centre horizon! Some people find a piece of stiff card, with a rectangular window cut into it, useful for selecting viewpoints. Hold it fairly close to your eye and you will soon see a portion of the landscape that pleases you and gives you a satisfying composition. Remember, too, scale: what might be uninteresting from where you first view it may be pictorially dramatic if you move to right or left.

Landscape can be enlivened by the weather. Dram-

atic clouds, rainstorms, or bursts of sunshine not only provide interesting subject-matter in themselves, but enliven the terrain beneath with light and shadow.

The compositional study above shows how interest lines converge on a farmhouse perched against a mountainside. The finished picture made from it appears overleaf, on page 8.

Abergynolwyn

This mountain farm at Abergynolwyn is a subject which composes naturally. The lines of mountains in the distance and the nearer slopes, together with the roadway, all lead the eye in to the centre of interest – the buildings. The strong movement down the slope of the mountain on which the farm is set continues to the right below it, but the eye does not run out of the picture; it is swung back by the slope of the near mountain on the right. The scale of the buildings is important when viewed from this position, for they seem to nestle naturally and to impart a rugged strength to the mountains.

Burford

I used grey sugar paper for this study which I made in the watermeadows on the edge of the beautiful old Cotswold town of Burford. I was attracted by the tall church spire, glimpsed between the willows growing along the banks of the Windrush, and the river leading neatly into the composition. The dark willow trees, particularly the trunks, contrast with the sunlight on the meadow beyond. In fact the whole foreground in shadow, including the trees, gives value to the generally light tone behind. Notice how I viewed the spire from off-centre, and have given more interest to the silhouette line of trees and spire.

Time of the day

Before you go sketching or painting outdoors, it is best to check on the weather forecast, for it will tell you not only what to wear, but probably help you to pre-select (outside your normal range of pastels) other colours which may come in handy. It will also help you choose where to go, for, if you already know your terrain, the knowledge that the sky above it will be clear or cloudy will influence the landscape.

I prefer to work when the sun is not at its zenith, for then shadows cast from buildings and trees are short. Early morning or late afternoon brings a drama to the landscape when the sun is relatively low, striking the clouds obliquely, throwing their shadows across hills and plains. Sunrise and sunset colour the landscape and sky with orange and purple hues – here the pastel medium is unrivalled for achieving luminosity.

I sometimes make as many as a dozen sketches and tonal drawings in one day of almost the same subject, observing the light and shade, and how the sun's position changes the shadows. In the next demonstration (pages 12–13) I was fortunate enough to catch the morning mist rising from the river: an atmospheric subject, well suited to a gentler approach with pastels than we have seen hitherto. This picture was painted in my studio from sketches made outdoors. The tonal study in charcoal on cartridge paper (opposite) establishes the composition.

Misty morning on the Windrush: demonstration

In this picture the mood and atmosphere of a misty morning in spring, with soft sunlight breaking through, is my main theme. The setting is a stretch of the River Windrush, in the Cotswold country. I have spent many pleasant hours on its banks at different seasons, and in varying weather conditions, so I arrived there early when I knew the mist would be rising.

Stage 1

I choose a lightish toned pearl Canson paper upon which to work, which will play an important part in the colour scheme throughout. I begin with some bold loose strokes of pale tints of ultramarine and yellow ochre, repeating the ultramarine in the water area, and use a cool grey for the distance. I put in loose marks of dark green-grey to suggest the reeds on the bank. I use pieces of pastel, about an inch long lengthways, without much pressure.

Stage 2

I continue to work with the green-grey for the tall trees to the left and a middle tone of the same colour between the two trees to the right and also behind and to the right of the left-hand trees. Mid-toned brown is applied for reeds on the distant river banks and left foreground, with more dark green-grey for reflections.

Stage 3

With the same colours I develop the shapes of the trees both to right and left. I now employ a mid-olive green, giving more warmth to the left-hand trees and bank

Tonal study in charcoal for the demonstration 'Misty morning on the Windrush' on the next two pages.

below and over to the right beneath the trees. The trunks of the trees are strengthened with dark brown, the same pastel being used for the river bank on the right. Two other distant tree trunks are added with a darker cool grey and a mid-warm grey.

Stage 4

I begin to develop more form with the same pastels but applying them with more pressure and rubbing them in

11

Stage 1

Stage 2

Stage 3

Stage 4

Stage 5 – the finished painting

More paintings are ruined by overworking than by underworking them; it is so easy to go on and on, introducing unnecessary detail and thereby losing the impact. With this in mind, I firmly draw in more detail in the reeds on the river banks, together with the reflections, and touch in more strongly the darker tones of all the trees. Lastly come the light touches of sap and grass greens and the bright highlights of yellow.

with my fingers in places, in the distant cool grey and the lighter reflections in the water and the sky. With the edge of the dark brown pastel I firmly draw in the willow tree branches on the right and strengthen further the branches of the two trees to the left, the reeds on the river bank in the left foreground, those on the right and the reflections in the water.

Stage 5 – the finished painting

This demonstration shows how pastels can be blended on the paper with the fingers, producing soft, pearly effects. But overblending can produce a woolliness that will render your picture insipid – also the colours will become muddy.

Skies

Always study the sky over your landscape. In many of my sketches and paintings the sky not only plays an important part through the effect of sunlight and shadow on the land, but provides me with 'backdrop' drama. In the sketch above the burst of sunlight on the lake only lasted a few minutes, and my sketch was finished a few moments after it had gone – yet I felt I had captured a worthwhile moment.

Cotswold lane in winter: demonstration

Winter is certainly not a time of year lacking in colour. The dramatic shapes of bare branches of trees seen against the sky offer fine subject-matter; and without foliage views become more open and subjects revealed that would be hidden in summer. The open tracery of bare trees or branches also can often provide fore-ground features to frame our subject, while a fall of

14

snow changes completely the normal tone values and, if accompanied by sunshine, gives beautiful colours in the shadows, chiefly blues and greys from the sky.

Stage 1 (page 15)

I am painting this demonstration in the studio using a lightish warm grey Canson paper, having stretched it beforehand. I dampen the paper with clear water and, with diluted Indian ink, wash it on with a large flat watercolour brush to give the background tones; the damp paper produces soft edges.

Stages 2–3 (page 16)

When the first wash is dry, I take a No. 8 nylon brush and, with undiluted Indian ink this time, boldly draw in the trunks and branches of the trees. For the foreground shadows and masses of twigs at top left I again use the flat brush and diluted ink, making them a little darker.

I block in the sky with pale tints of cerulean and ultramarine blue pastel, together with a light warm grey to provide an effect of broken colour. I also use a cerulean blue for the snow under the trees. I apply a darker tone of the same grey as in the sky to the background, together with a couple of blue-greys (one of them about the same tonal strength as the warm grey, the other a little darker) to provide the shadows of the foreground.

Stage 4

I add the lightest tint of yellow ochre to the sunlit snow in the foreground and stronger yellow ochre and burnt sienna to the hedge behind the trees on the left and the foreground to left and right. A middle tone of burnt umber is dragged over the tops of the trees to the left, using the pastel flat along its length, to suggest masses

Stage 1

of twigs. I apply deep tones of grey and olive greens of the same strength to the near tree to the right, also to those on the left, together with a touch of lighter olive to the right. Some dark burnt umber is added to the trunks.

Detail (page 16)

This same-size detail shows how the grain of the paper and the dark washes show through, giving my pastel strokes brilliance and vibrancy.

Stage 5 – the finished painting (page 17)

Using the same colours, I work over the whole picture, concentrating chiefly on the foreground to create the effect of sunlight from the left. The shadows cast by the trees to the left are an important feature; I use them to describe the ruts in the snow and the rough surface textures. I apply a touch of red to the figure to contrast with the cool colours of the snow, and put in touches of light tints on the trees to indicate snow lodged in the branches.

Stage 2

Stage 3

Stage 4

Detail

Stage 5 – the finished painting

Tonal studies

Whenever possible I try to make tonal sketches like the ones on these pages before I start to work with pastel. Such studies help me to find the best composition and also to determine the balance of my picture, so that the centre of interest is in the correct place. Normally I use charcoal on white cartridge (these studies are in that medium). Conté or soft pencil are suitable – use any medium, in fact, which will give you the results you seek.

The Bridge,
Lower Slaughter:
demonstration

Despite its rather off-putting name, this is one of the most attractive of the Cotswold villages, nestling as it does in a sheltered valley in the wolds. The houses' reflections in the clear placid stream which flows through the village appealed to me, so I placed myself opposite them, then worked this picture to its finished stage in my studio.

Stage 1 (page 20)

With a dark autumnal brown pastel I draw in the main shapes on light grey Canson Moonstone paper. I use the edge of the pastel stick to indicate the outlines of the buildings, while for the trees and reflections I apply it generally with the side.

Stage 1

Stage 2

Stage 3

Stage 4

Stage 2

I apply the light tones of ultramarine, yellow ochre and red grey for the sky, again using the pastels flat. With the lengths of the pastels I apply dark green-grey in the shadows of the tall trees to the left, the small one below and the dark tree to the right. A middle-toned sap green gives me the lighter side of the tall tree, the smaller one below and the grass verges. Two mid-tones each of green and blue-grey are used for the distant trees, with a touch of light grass green.

Stage 3

I now lay in lightly mid-brown for the roofs of the cottages to the left, with a darker tone of the same colour on the shadowed gable. Similarly I put in the roof of the other cottage, using mid-raw umber for the wall in shadow and light brown for the sunlit gables and the chimneys. Mid-brown is applied along the wall towards the dark tree which is further darkened with olive green. I use mid-olive green on the tall tree and on the dark one to the right. Light tones of sap and grass greens brighten up the grass areas.

Stage 5 – the finished painting

Stage 4

Using the same colours, I apply them overall, this time with more pressure, and add more detail. I use light brown for the sunlit cottage walls on the left and the stone wall in the water below, with middle sap green on bushes in the gardens. I develop the water reflections lightly with the same colours I used for the trees and buildings above, making downward strokes. I apply light ultramarine under the bridge. I add a little mid-toned red grey to the roof of the middle cottage on the left, then put in the figures. The pathway near the figures is indicated with light and darker red greys.

Stage 5 – the finished painting

The picture is now worked up all over. Rubbing-in with finger or thumb (see page 23) in the water conveys a smooth effect. The foreground reeds and wild flowers are stated, but I am careful not to overwork this area as it would detract from the central interest of the picture – the cottages.

Artefacts in landscape

As in the previous demonstration the centre of interest in a landscape can be a group of buildings – in fact it is hard to find a landscape devoid of any man-made artefact or building. Such artefacts make an admirable foil to the natural scene, with their contrasting textures to woodland, trees, grasses and streams. The sketch

above, painted on grey Canson paper, is of Upper Slaughter, the neighbouring village to the one in the demonstration on pages 19–21. I keep all my sketches and go through them from time to time, working up those that please me most into exhibition pictures.

Rubbing-in techniques

While pastel is very effective when the sticks are used directly onto the tooth or grain of the paper support, as in the sketches in this book, their effectiveness can be enhanced by contrasting the direct marks with blending or rubbing-in. Water areas and soft foliage can be treated in this way; make your marks on the paper with one or more tints and lines according to what you see, then smooth the pigment into the grain of the paper with thumb, fingertip or a pointed stump or rolled-up newspaper. A few judicious strokes over this rubbed-in area with stick pastel will sharpen up features – such as ripples in water, branches of trees, reeds, grasses.

But care must be taken not to overwork this technique, otherwise the painting will become woolly. Techniques are a means to an end, never the end in itself. You will see how I have used a mixture of direct work and blending in the demonstrations, but have not allowed the rubbing-in to dominate the overall crispness of the finished pictures.

I tend to blend or rub-in mostly in the water and sky areas of my pictures which, by their nature, tend to be soft and amorphous.

Mixed media

In the demonstration on pages 15–17 I first applied Indian ink in dilute washes, and then undiluted, to prepare my picture before painting over it in pastel. This is but one way of combining other media with pastel. Charcoal conté, watercolour, gouache, acrylic, waterfast felt-tip pens can all be used in combination with pastel, but only at the preliminary stages. One point to remember: any medium that contains grease or oil will never mix with pastel!

In my sketches I will often block in or outline my subject with coarse or wedge-tipped felt pens. The ink dries immediately and takes the pastel painting that follows over it well. Sometimes I will leave this preliminary drawing showing through rather than accent the picture with dark pastel. Remember, if applied vigorously pastel will cover up any underdrawing, for its pigments are opaque.

Some pastel painters will go so far as to paint a complete underpainting in watercolour; then apply pastels over it. Some beautiful effects and textures can be obtained in this way, but the beginner should be wary of the technique before he or she has mastered the different methods of handling pastels.

View from
Malvern (1)

The two views near Malvern on this page and on page 25 illustrate several points about observing the weather to make compositions more interesting. In the sketch above I waited until a shaft of sunlight illuminated the field in front of me and also caught the roof of the barn beyond it, thus providing me with a centre of interest otherwise lacking. A lively sky above it completes the interest.

View from Malvern (2)

In this sketch the fence in the foreground dramatises the sunlit field beyond it, the pathway drawing my eye towards the village spire in the middle distance, also lit by sunlight. Both these sketches are simple but effective; yet they would be dull without the advent of the sunshine/shadow patterns.

Pointillist techniques

Among the most effective techniques we can use with pastel painting is to apply the pastel stick to the support or paper by 'dabbing' the end of it rather than by dragging it across the surface. This technique can be related to the discoveries of the Impressionist and Post-Impressionist painters of nineteenth-century France. Instead of painting in brushstrokes the colour of their observations they found that, by analysing colours scientifically, they could place small spots of one colour against those of another, the observed result being a third colour – the one they wished the onlooker to 'see'. The resulting pictures had a vibrant effect not achieved by any other means and can be seen at their most effective in the works or Seurat and Signac. We now know that the evidence on which the theory was based is not strictly scientific – nevertheless, this pointillist technique has found favour with many painters, and can provide a way of rendering a subject unlike any other.

Pastels are ideal for experimenting with this technique. In the demonstration that follows I have not stuck strictly to the 'scientific' aspect, but have demonstrated how a painting can be built up in this way.

First of all, do stretch your paper over newspaper wadding, as I have explained earlier (page 3). This will allow you to make each small mark without fracturing the pastel stick. Your dots or marks should not follow any particular direction, nor should they be of the same size or shape, as this will make your finished result look monotonous.

Worcestershire lane: pointillist demonstration

Stage 1 (page 27)

For this demonstration I choose again the warm, light grey Canson paper called Moonstone. First I draw in the outlines of the main features and indicate the position of the shadows across the road and grass verges.

Stage 2 (page 28)

Applying the pastels in dots I begin with the sky, using light tints of ultramarine, yellow ochre, cerulean blue, grey and red-grey, together with a mid-toned blue-grey. I then continue with three tones of blue-grey and a dark purple grey for the distant trees. These cool lines are especially helpful when I begin to consider the warm colours of the buildings against them in the next stage of the painting.

Stage 3

Using a number of warm colours such as autumnal brown, a touch or two of vermilion, crimson, Prussian blue and mid-purple grey, I establish a generally warm tone for the roofs of the farmhouse and the buildings below. For the roof of the barn to the left I apply mid and light tones of ochre, with light vermilion. For the darker tones on the shadowed side I use purple grey, Prussian blue and crimson. The shadowed walls of the farmhouse are treated with a warm grey, as used in the sky, and with pale yellow ochre for the light gables.

The trees are stippled in with mid-tones of brown for the twigs and dark brown for trunks and branches. I use open treatment for the twigs, filling in more solidly the

Stage 1

trunks and branches and using mid and light yellow ochre for the sunlit parts of the trunk on the right. Dark and mid-green grey with dark olive green are used for the ivy. These same dark greens are repeated at the base of the hedge to the left and in a more open way for a suggestion of the shadows on the grass verges. For the sunny greens I use light shades of grass green and terre verte.

Stage 4

I continue to apply more dotted pigments to the light and shadow both on the road and grass verges. A range of dark and mid-tones of olive and sap greens gives me the shadows whilst light tints of sap, grass and yellow greens with a few touches of terre verte produce the light. The sunlit passages on the road are a repetition of the sky colours (less than blues), with red-grey mid-tone and a touch or two of dark purple brown.

Stage 2

Stage 3

Stage 4

Detail

Detail

This same-size detail shows to good effect the shapes of the marks and also how the neutral-toned paper 'binds' them together. You will notice how the actual colours I use are much stronger in hue than those I would employ for conventional sketching and painting.

Stage 5 – the finished painting

Stage 5 – the finished painting

I continue working on the foreground area, using the same colours as before, but covering the paper with more dots and making these generally larger in the near foreground to give an effect of recession. I develop more light and shade contrast on the road with light yellow ochre and dark shades of brown and purple grey. I leave a certain amount of paper showing throughout the work to provide harmony.

Fixing pastels

It is possible to spray a liquid fixative over pastel paintings in order to prevent smudging of the work. However I rarely resort to this as it causes a considerable lowering of tones and loss of freshness. A freshly painted pastel has a certain bloom which resembles the surface of a fresh, ripe peach. This is entirely lost when the painting is sprayed.

It is sound practice to lay in the basic underlying tones of a picture, spray them with fixative and continue working over, treating it as a form of underpainting. An advantage of this approach is that any further application of the pastel over the sprayed passages is unaffected by the colours beneath, with little or no mixing taking place.

The best method of protecting a pastel painting when it is finished is to frame it beneath glass as soon as possible. It will then preserve all its bloom of fresh colour and texture.

Storing pastel paintings

If it is not possible to frame all our pastel pictures, then we need to store them in such a way that they will not be damaged. The danger from smudging is, of course, the chief concern, but this is not so great a problem as many perhaps might think, providing certain basic precautions are taken. Work may be stored placed flat in a drawer with sheets of tissue paper between the pictures and pins or paper clips holding all together, or holding each picture firmly to its protecting sheet of tissue.

My own method of storage is to fix to the wall a pair of narrow shelf brackets (of the type used in erecting multiple shelves). Bulldog clips are slid along the arms of these by means of their ring attachments, my pictures being clipped in position and suspended below.

Presentation

Pastel paintings look best when they are surrounded with a double mount, the inner one cut smaller than the outer. These keep the picture well away from the glass, which should always cover the front of any pastel framing to protect it from dust and accidental damage to the surface.

Before the picture is set in its frame, loose particles of pastel should be removed from its surface by tapping the corner of the board on which it is mounted sharply on the floor, or flicking the loose support on the back lightly with the fingers.

Barmouth. *This quick sketch (opposite page) of the sun breaking through to illuminate the sea was made from my car. I always keep in the car a board and a few sheets of paper clipped onto it, together with a box of basic pastels in flour, colours which I habitually use, so that, if I see an attractive view or natural effect, I can stop and record it.*

ACKNOWLEDGEMENTS

Text, drawings and paintings by Aubrey Phillips

Series editor: Peter D. Johnson

Text, illustrations, arrangement and typography
copyright © Search Press Limited 1984

First published in Great Britain in 1984 by Search Press Limited,
Wellwood, North Farm Road, Tunbridge Wells, Kent TN2 3DR

Reprinted 1987, 1989

U.S. Artists Materials Trade Distributor:
Winsor & Newton, Inc.
11, Constitution Avenue, P. O. Box 1396, Piscataway, NJ08855-1396

Canadian Distributors:
Anthes Universal Limited
341 Heart Lake Road South, Brampton, Ontario L6W 3K8

Australian Distributors:
Jasco Pty. Limited
937-941 Victoria Road, West Ryde, N.S.W. 2114

New Zealand Distributors:
Caldwell Wholesale Ltd
Wellington and Auckland

UK ISBN 0 85532 533 X

Made and printed in Spain by A. G. Elkar, S. Coop.
Autonomía, 71 - 48012-Bilbao - Spain.

The beach at Aberdovey. *After I made my pastel
sketch of this sunlit beach I went over it here and there
with fine felt-tip pen in order to strengthen the outlines
and pick out detail.*